Early Foundations in the Bible

Moses
and the Mighty Plagues

John and Kim Walton
Illustrated by Alice Craig

Chariot Books is an imprint of David C. Cook Publishing Co.
David C. Cook Publishing Co., Elgin, Illinois 60120
David C. Cook Publishing Co., Weston, Ontario

MOSES AND THE MIGHTY PLAGUES
© 1986 by John and Kim Walton for the text and Alice Craig for the illustrations.
All rights reserved. Except for brief excerpts for review purposes, no part of this book may be reproduced or used in any form without written permission from the publisher.

Cover design by Barbara Sheperd Tillman

Based on Exodus 7—12

First printing, 1986
Printed in the United States of America
90 89 88 87 86   5 4 3 2 1
ISBN 1-55513-041-0
LC 86-70676

A Word to Parents

As a Bible professor, I find that too much of my time is spent "unteaching"—trying to reverse incorrect notions that students have picked up along the way from children's storybooks or well-meaning Sunday school materials. Naturally we simplify stories for children; they can hardly be expected to grasp all that is involved in Scripture, or even understand all the words. But early exposure to Bible stories, correctly interpreted and applied, provides a good basis for later learning.

The Early Foundations in the Bible series is committed to the authority of the biblical text. The illustrations, brightly colored and two dimensional, are historically and biblically accurate, as far as the detail allows. The interpretation of some stories may differ a little from that with which you're familiar; the notes on the last page of each book explain the biblical basis for the story. These notes, while far more detailed than your preschooler needs, will help you understand the background of the story and answer questions your child might have.

We pray that your child will enjoy these stories and grow up well versed in God's Word.

John H. Walton

The people of Israel were slaves in the land of Egypt.

God told Moses to lead the Israelites out of Egypt to the land he had promised to them.

But Pharaoh, the king of Egypt, wouldn't let the Israelites go.

Moses told Pharaoh that God would send plagues on Egypt if Pharaoh didn't let the Israelites leave.

First, all the water turned to blood.

Then there were frogs, then gnats,

and then flies everywhere.

But Pharaoh still wouldn't let the people go.

Cattle died,

and Egyptians got sick.

and then darkness came in the daytime.

**And Pharaoh *still*
wouldn't let the Israelites go.**

Then came the last plague:
God told Pharaoh
that the firstborn in every family
would die.

When the last plague came, Pharaoh finally let the Israelites go.

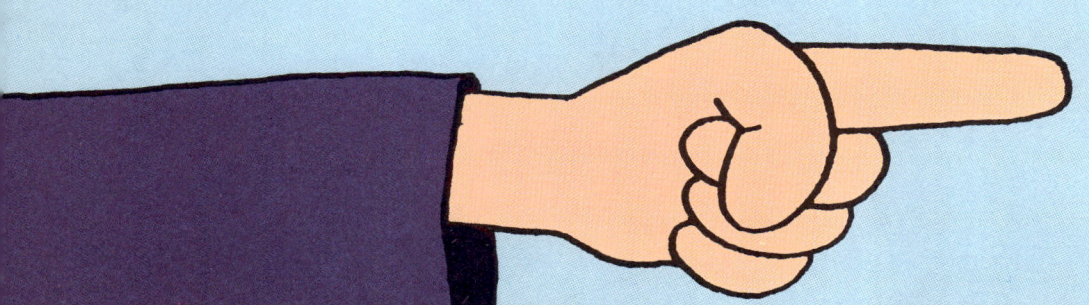

God had delivered his people, just as he promised.

**God is so strong
that nothing can stop him
from keeping his promises.**

Did You Realize . . .

(These notes from the author are for you, the parent, offering further explanation and interpretation of the text. While much of the information is far beyond what your preschooler could understand, it can equip you to answer questions that your child might raise.)

Pages 4, 5
This illustration was drawn from an Egyptian tomb painting from about the time the Israelites were in Egypt.

Page 6
God spoke to Moses from a burning bush (Exodus 3:2).

Page 12
This was a threatening first plague because Egypt, a farming society, was dependent on the Nile River.

Page 25
The Israelite families were also in danger from this plague, but God gave instructions for putting the blood of a slaughtered lamb on the doorposts to prevent their children from being slain.